The Gift of Words

Having the Right Words at the Right Time

Anne S. French

ISBN: 1-4196-6905-2
ISBN-13: 978-1419669057

Visit www.booksurge.com to order additional copies.

Acknowledgments

I want to thank the following people for the help they gave me in the creation of this book: my dear friend Kimberle Farver, who gave me unwavering support and was there years ago when we first coined the phrase "Gift of Words." A special thanks to Donald Fuller, Lindsey Johnson, and Bill Taylor for their photographic and graphics contribution. My heartfelt gratitude to Dennis Grindle for his wise counsel on this endeavor as well as others. Kelley Norwine, a friend whose honest feedback I trust implicitly. My incredibly thoughtful nephew, Steve Poore, who gave me direction on how to finally get this book off the ground. The stellar publishing team at BookSurge, who reinforced me every step of the way. I could not have asked for a more conscientious and knowledgeable group of professionals to help me launch my book.

And finally, my sweet David. You have been my gyroscope, keeping me balanced and levelheaded throughout this process. I thank you for your immense creative input and unconditional love. You have no idea how much you mean to me. I could not have done this without you.

CONTENTS

Page

INTRODUCTION – The Gift of Words   3

I.   SOMEWHAT AWKWARD SITUATIONS

How to Respond When You Are Being Approached by
    Someone with Whom You Do Not Want to Interact   6

How to Apologize When You Have Forgotten
    Someone's Birthday or Special Occasion   8

How to be Gracious When Your Friend Gets the Job
    Instead of You   9

How to Respond When You Do Not Like the Food   10

How to Respond Initially to an Unappealing Blind Date   11

How to Respond to Someone at a Funeral   12

How to Tell Someone They Have an Offensive Habit   15

How to Respond When You Have Made a Cultural Faux Pas   16

How to Avoid an Unwanted Goodnight Kiss   17

II. DAY-TO-DAY STRESSORS

How to Respond When You Are Late to an
    Important Meeting   20

How to Leave a Prospective Employer with a
    Positive Impression After Your Interview   21

How to Turn Down a Request from a Neighbor   22

How to Turn Down a Solicitation for Money   24

How to Say No to a Volunteer Situation   25

How to Tell Your Kids No at the Store   26

How to Approach a Colleague about Troubling Behavior   28

How to Explain to Your Boss What is Troubling You
    About a Colleague   30

How to Tell a Colleague Her Clothes Are Too Sexy   32

How to Get Someone's Undivided Attention   34

How to Engage in Conversation with a Stranger   36

How to State a Differing Viewpoint   37

How to Respond to a Disapproving Parent   38

How to Respond to a Friend Who has Experienced a
    Great Disappointment   40

How to Respond When You Encounter an Ex in Public   42

How to Respond to Receiving Unsatisfactory Service   44

III.   <u>EMOTIONALLY INTENSE SITUATIONS</u>

How to Respond to a Verbally Abusive Person   46

How to Respond When Meeting Your Ex-Spouse to
    Discuss Visitation or Custody Arrangements   48

How to Ask for a Raise   50

How to Respond When You Do Not Get the Job   52

How to Tell Someone You Do Not Want to Drink
    Alcohol or Do Drugs   55

How to Graciously Back Out of a Promise   57

How to Respond to a Racial Slur   59

How to Graciously Refuse a Marriage Proposal   60

How to Back Out of a Wedding   62

Author's Note

One of the benefits I've gained in sharing my Gift of Words and helping people find answers to hard questions is a sense of peaceful purpose. With that in mind, I have included my original art. I hope it helps you find the serenity that comes when you find that the simple truth is all you need.

THE GIFT OF WORDS

Years ago when I was working as a court reporter, a colleague of mine approached me and asked for my help. Apparently, she had come up against a demanding and bullying lawyer who had yelled at her for getting a transcript to him late. My friend, Jessica, explained to me that she had been working for days on this 300-page transcript and had, in fact, met the deadline the lawyer had requested. It was the delivery service that had caused the delay, not Jessica.

Jessica shared with me the phone call she had received from the angry lawyer. He did not let her get a word in edgewise. He called her incompetent and irresponsible and threatened that this was not the last she had heard about this fiasco. She was literally in tears relaying to me how the conversation had gone, how helpless, embarrassed, and humiliated she felt. Her biggest frustration came from not having the right words to say to the attorney when she needed them. She had been so caught off guard, she came away totally defeated, believing the lawyer's harsh words.

What I learned at that moment from Jessica is how powerless we feel when we do not have the right words to say at the right time. No matter the situation, being unprepared with comebacks, or not knowing the response we want to give when we are feeling intimidated or bullied, leaves us feeling frustrated and demeaned.

I went back to Jessica a few days after the incident and told her she would never have to feel so caught off guard again because I had come up with a phrase that she could use. I gave her the "Gift of Words" – a response that could give Jessica satisfaction as well as allow her to keep her professionalism. The words I suggested Jessica use if a similar incident ever arose again – and I have shared this phrase with countless other people who find themselves at a loss for words – were, **"You must be speaking to me that way because you think you can. Well, you can't, and until you take a kinder tone, this conversation is over!"**

This book will give you the words you need for many difficult situations. Look at them. Learn them. Memorize them if it will help you feel the power of language when you are at a loss for words and need them most.

I.

SOMEWHAT AWKWARD SITUATIONS

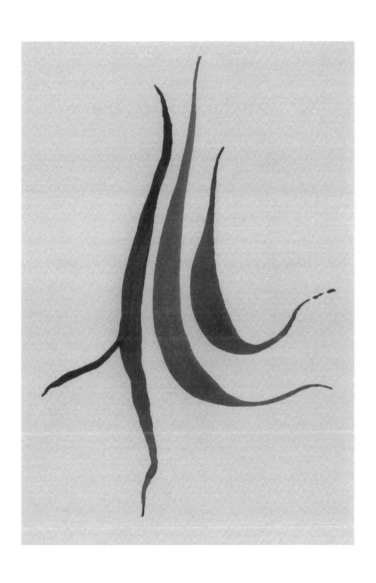

How to Respond When You Are Being Approached by Someone with Whom You Do Not Want to Interact

Scenario

I was sitting in a club with a couple of girlfriends, trying to make conversation over the loud music. As I scanned the room for interesting faces, I saw someone approaching. He wasn't bad. I just wasn't interested. Now I have a way out before it gets really awkward.

Words to Say

"I'm not going to pretend. I'm not interested in getting to know you. Thanks for coming by and introducing yourself, but don't let me keep you."

Why They Work

Our need to be liked and not wanting to hurt someone's feelings puts us at a distinct disadvantage in social situations. That is why the words are precise and unambiguous. He will get the hint without being devastated.

How to Apologize When You Have Forgotten Someone's Birthday or Special Occasion

Scenario

It could be your grandmother's 75th birthday. It might be your husband's sales award luncheon. It may even be your best friend's baby shower. We all forget special occasions from time to time and have to suffer the embarrassment of apologizing.

Words to Say

"How I could forget the birthday of someone who is so special to me is beyond comprehension. Please know how sorry I am for this oversight, and let me know what I can do to make it up to you."

Why They Work

Your good intentions and thoughtfulness remain intact with this statement. How could someone not forgive you when you show such a willingness to make amends? Make good on your promise to make things right.

How to be Gracious When Your Friend Gets the Job Instead of You

Scenario

In this fierce job market, sometimes we find ourselves competing with close friends for the same job. Recently, I found myself in this very uncomfortable position. When I looked critically at my own qualifications for the job, I felt confident that I should be their first choice for filling the position. I learned my friend felt the same way about her own qualifications and skills. It really became more of letting the chips fall where they may. No backbiting or sabotage. But they fell her way, and I accepted that.

Words to Say

"I am so glad that if I couldn't get the job, it went to someone so deserving. They are lucky to have such a talented person in that position. I know you'll do a great job."

Why They Work

There is something truly gratifying that comes from wishing someone well… and meaning it. By being gracious, you earn respect and admiration from those who see it, and you ultimately have a quiet sense of pride in how you handled a tough situation.

How to Respond When You Do Not Like the Food

Scenario

You have been invited to someone's house for dinner. You're looking forward to it. The mood is warm and congenial as you enter the house, and you notice the hostess putting the finishing touches on her oyster mousse with sautéed beets. What do you do? We've all been in situations where we just can't eat the food being served. There are ways to draw the attention away from what you won't eat to what you appreciate about the dining experience.

Words to Say

"I can see you have gone to a lot of trouble preparing this meal. It all looks delicious. Unfortunately, I can't eat spinach (or lima beans, oysters, etc.), so please forgive me for not taking any on my plate."

Why They Work

Acknowledging the effort one has put forth preparing a meal is the number one priority here. The detail of why you "can't eat" something is unnecessary and crass. By being properly enthusiastic about the rest of the dining experience (the presentation, for example), the hostess will more than likely forget and forgive your initial refusal.

How to Respond Initially to an Unappealing Blind Date

Scenario

At one time or another we have all found ourselves on blind dates. We anticipate the worst and often find ourselves pleasantly surprised. Just remember that being gracious, no matter what the circumstance, is the best approach. These words break the ice and make an awkward situation a little less so.

Words to Say

"Hi. I'm happy to meet you. I have to admit, I'm always so anxious about this kind of meeting where you just don't know what to expect. Aren't you?"

Why They Work

Have integrity by responding with courtesy and good humor. Whether he's a nail-biter, bad dresser, or smoker, your date is for an evening, not a lifetime. Look for those admirable traits that may be hidden on first glance. Initiate conversation where you make the most of your brief time together without leaving the impression you are open to future invitations.

How to Respond to Someone at a Funeral

Scenario

I was quietly waiting my turn to give my condolences to the bereaved widow, a family friend I had known for years. I realized I didn't have anything different or unique to offer in letting her know how sorry I was for her loss. My words were sincere, just not particularly helpful. That's when I tried to imagine what I might really need if this happened to me.

Words to Say

"I am so sorry about your husband's passing. I can't imagine what you're going through, but you have my heartfelt sympathy. I will call you soon, after things settle down a bit, to see where you can use my help."

or

"I know a little of what you must be going through. My _____ passed away a short time ago. You have my heartfelt sympathy. I will call you soon, after things settle down a bit, to see where I can be of help."

Why They Work

Whether you have suffered your own personal loss or simply attended funerals of distant relatives, we all find it awkward to talk about death. These two examples are tailor made for each kind of event. The universal statement we are all inclined to make, "Call me if you need anything," is not particularly helpful. It sounds empty. By using these statements, you show a willingness to give help down the road when the grieving person may be all but forgotten.

How to Tell Someone They Have an Offensive Habit

Scenario

It might be the girl in the office, your favorite teacher, or the elderly gentleman down the street who drops by to visit from time to time. We all do our best to avoid people with disgusting smells, be it body odor, bad breath, or excessive perfume. But they're out there, and they need to be told! Here's a way to broach this very touchy subject without devastating the recipient too much.

Words to Say

"It is difficult for me to mention this to you, even though I think you'd want to know. I would if it were me. I've noticed a strong scent when you are close to me that you need to be aware of. I hope it's okay that I brought this up."

Why They Work

Of all the things we confront people about, this may be one of the most difficult. That's because it's so personal. No matter how tactful we are, no matter how much finesse we use, we are going to embarrass someone with this statement. Even if it's hard to hear, they will be glad you told them…and so will others.

How to Respond When You Have Made a Cultural Faux Pas

Scenario

I feel sure I've offended my way across the world. Not on purpose, of course. But when traveling to foreign countries, I'm often a little unsure of the customs and behavior that are appropriate. It may be wearing a head covering in a church, or not offering your left hand in greeting. Learn the habits of the locals. Respect the cultural differences. If you make mistakes, these words may help you save face.

Words to Say

"Please forgive me. I should have known _____ (to cover my head with a scarf in your church). Thank you for helping me learn about your customs. I will certainly never make that mistake again."

Why They Work

Asking for forgiveness is one of the broadest forms of apology you can make. By thanking them for teaching you their customs, you make the situation less awkward and help relieve any embarrassment. Now, hopefully, you will be given a chance to make things right.

How to Avoid an Unwanted Goodnight Kiss

Scenario

Boy, we've all been in this position at one time or another in our life. Whether you are a bumbling teenager or a bumbling fifty-year-old, it never gets easier. You both stand there not knowing exactly what to say. You start to offer your hand, and you see him leaning in to plant a big 'ole sloppy one on you. Now what?

Words to Say

"Let me interrupt us right here. I'm really not ready to get any closer tonight, and I want to thank you for a wonderful evening."

Why They Work

Using the word "interrupt" is like physically putting up your hand as a stop sign. You make your message clear. Your explanation is thoughtful but to the point. By saying "and" instead of "but," you acknowledge the evening appropriately without negating your first and most important comment.

II.

DAY-TO-DAY STRESSORS

How to Respond When You Are Late to an Important Meeting

Scenario

It's been on your calendar for a month. Everyone knows that all the executives will be attending. It's not that you forgot. You simply got started late. The traffic was worse than usual. It's always something. But don't start making excuses. Nobody cares *why* you're late; they just care that you *are* late. So have a little dignity with how you handle this embarrassing situation.

Words to Say

"I have no excuse. I know how important this meeting is, and you have my profound apology for arriving late. I'll be sure and get anything I missed from _____ after the meeting is over."

Why They Work

Hold yourself accountable without making excuses, and you will gain respect. It shows initiative and responsibility when you offer a way to get what you may have missed. Then don't let it happen again.

How to Leave a Prospective Employer with a Positive Impression After Your Interview

Scenario

You have been looking forward to this interview for weeks. You've been planning your strategy, preparing your words in anticipation of meeting the CFO of this company. Besides impressing the executive with your talents and expertise as well as your interest in the company, consider going one step further. As your meeting comes to a close, leave a lasting impression by using these words.

Words to Say

"Let me just say, once again, that if I get the job, I will show initiative and a willingness to learn everything I need to do the job right. You will never regret that you gave me this chance."

Why They Work

A powerful closing remark can make all the difference. These are the very things an employer thinks about as she interviews prospective employees. Allay her doubts. Be memorable. Don't forget that you only have one chance to make a good first impression, so let it also be the last thing she remembers about you. Very few people think to do this.

How to Turn Down a Request from a Neighbor

Scenario

It seems that almost every day we are approached by friends or family members with something they want us to do. You might be asked to watch the kids for an hour while they run an errand, or requested to make your famous peach cobbler that everyone loves for the potluck dinner next week. They make it sound like an innocent request, no big deal. But it is a big deal if you really don't want to do it. Escape their clutches, if you dare, with these words.

Words to Say

"I'm afraid I won't be able to watch the kids this afternoon because I have other commitments. I hope you will understand. Perhaps there will be another opportunity in the future for me to help out."

Why They Work

This is short and direct, but leaves an opening for how you want to handle future events. You do not want to alienate your friends and neighbors by turning down their requests too often. On the other hand, it is absolutely okay for you to say no when you have other commitments.

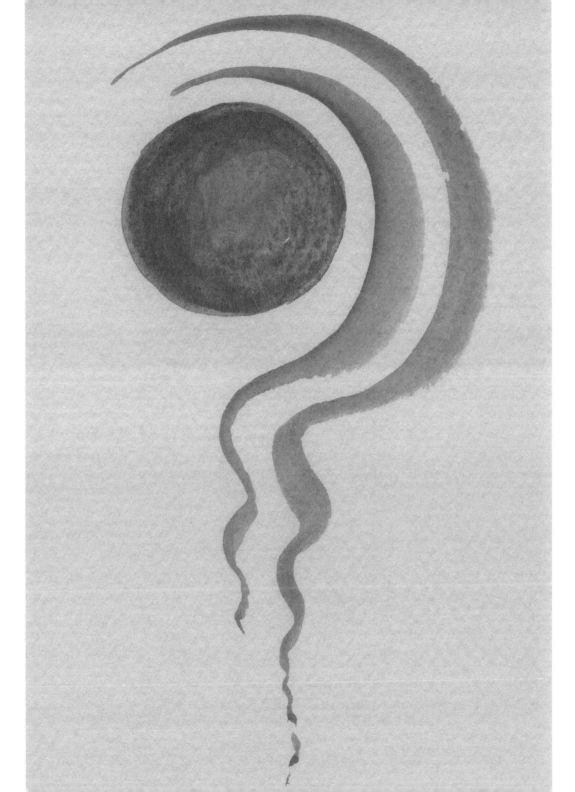

How to Turn Down a Solicitation for Money

Scenario

Requests for contributions come in many forms. You get unsolicited phone calls when you least expect it. You get mailers filling your mailbox and flyers under your windshield in parking lots. You get knocks on your door at dinnertime. You are approached by your kids for all kinds of altruistic causes at school. No one is safe from this onslaught of needs and requests, so have your words ready.

Words to Say

"It is most difficult to say no, but at this time I have other financial priorities that come first. Please understand. I believe in your cause. I'm just not in a position to make a contribution."

Why They Work

By talking about priorities, you leave little room for discussion, thus no one takes offense. Charity requests are some of the hardest ones to ignore. We hem and haw trying to think of an acceptable turn-down, but guilt still drives us to donate even when we really can't afford it or just don't want to. I personally believe that you can be kind and direct at the same time.

How to Say No to a Volunteer Situation

Scenario

Sometimes volunteering to do something doesn't really feel like volunteering. We may feel the subtle tug of coercion, guilt, or peer pressure. No matter. Decide if you really want to commit your time, energy, services, money, house, car, etc. If you need an out, here are the words that might help.

Words to Say

"It's important you understand that my saying no is not a reflection of my lack of interest, simply a lack of time. I have priorities that must come first. I'll be happy to contact you if my situation changes."

Why They Work

Peer pressure weighs on all of us. By stating specifically that the problem lies in that you lack time, not interest, you eliminate the need to defend yourself any further. People can't argue your priorities, so make this a gentle response.

How to Tell Your Kids No at the Store

Scenario

You're in a toy store trying to shop as fast as possible for the birthday gift for the five-year-old who lives down the street. Your two little ones are hanging on your shorts and swinging from the cart when the whining and wheedling start. You know what I'm talking about…and you don't even have to be a parent to experience this. You can be an aunt, an uncle, a grandmother, a cousin, a mother-in-law. Children pull this on all of us. Show your love without pulling out your pocketbook.

Words to Say

"Just because you see that toy does not mean you get it. I want to see you behave for me like I know you can – no yelling, no crying – and you can choose an activity you'd like us to do together when we get home."

Why They Work

By offering a clear, positive statement of what you expect their behavior to be, you have eliminated room for argument. Children have unfailing perseverance and an endless supply of mind-numbing questions to wear you down. Your alternative offer of an activity you can do together when you get home is a great negotiation tool. Be sure and follow through with your promise.

How to Approach a Colleague about Troubling Behavior

Scenario

You can already feel the butterflies, the physical symptoms we suffer when we are about to confront someone. Even the most confident, savvy, articulate person can become nervous and verbally clumsy when she has to approach someone about a problem. We all admire those who do it well, who know what to say without devastating the recipient of the criticism. When you ultimately clear the air, working together can be so much better.

Words to Say

"I have tried to work with you for a while now, but I feel you just are not receptive to my help or ideas. Perhaps I'm reading you wrong, but I feel you have been particularly overbearing (negative, gossiping, lazy, etc.). I'd really like your suggestion on how we might resolve this since we work so closely together."

Why They Work

Avoidance is the universal trap…but we can only do it for so long. Ultimately, we have to confront the things that really bother us. This is particularly true in a work environment where we spend so many hours. By stating that you may be wrong about your perception of the problem helps your coworker save face. You will also get a better outcome with this collaborative suggestion of solving the problem together.

How to Explain to Your Boss What is Troubling You
About a Colleague

Scenario

When you have been working with people for a while, you get a feel for how they interact with others, how they approach problems, what their work ethic is. When a conflict or problem becomes persistent or escalates and the person avoids talking with you about how to resolve it, it may be time to see your supervisor. Keeping peace in the workplace while staying productive can be a challenge if there's underlying discord. Approach your colleague first to try to solve the problem. If that doesn't work, here are some words to get your boss' attention.

Words to Say

"I have tried to work with _____ for a while now, but I feel he/she is just not receptive to my help or ideas. Perhaps you have a suggestion for how I might better deal with his/her bossiness (negativity, gossiping, laziness, etc.)."

Why They Work

Retain your professionalism by keeping your conversations about coworkers confidential; otherwise, it will reflect badly on you. If you have tried your best to work with a difficult coworker (by trying the strategy I mention on the previous page) and have gotten no results, it may be time to see the boss. Keep your comments focused on the problem areas, where you want help. It may ultimately require the three of you meeting together to get the problem solved.

How to Tell a Colleague Her Clothes Are Too Sexy

Scenario

We all know women who dress this way. We see them at the mall, in church, at clubs, at family get-togethers. But when the provocative dresser enters the workplace, it's a very hard thing to confront. You don't want to step on one's style, fashion sense, or personal statement, which is exactly what you might be accused of doing if you confront them about the way they dress. You'll feel anxious and uncomfortable if you are the one in a position to address this problem, so be prepared with the right words.

Words to Say

"Please, _____, do not take offense. I need you to dress more modestly when we are working together. It is distracting to our clients and sends the wrong message. I value your help, but this needs to change if we are going to work together."

Why They Work

When discussing sensitive issues, balance the message with how the person is valued. Let's be honest. Women know when they are being provocative and attracting attention. It is often done with care and deliberation. But if we dress this way in the workplace, we lose credibility and won't be taken seriously. It is a valid argument to suggest client distraction. It also can affect the bottom line if clients are too uncomfortable and stop doing business with you altogether.

How to Get Someone's Undivided Attention

Scenario

Have you heard the old saying, "Timing is everything"? It can apply to so many situations. Timing affects everything we do, whether it's finding the perfect house exactly when you sell your old one, or running in to someone you haven't seen in a long time that you've been meaning to call. That's why the strategy of asking for specific time when you want to discuss something important is such a critical element. It sets the stage for really substantive discussion.

Words to Say

"When I can get your undivided attention for about ten minutes, there is an important matter I would like to discuss with you. I look forward to you getting back to me."

Why They Work

Setting time limits for discussion is critical if you want a receptive listener. We often over-sell, over-talk, or over-explain our side of an argument. Be direct and to the point. Also, by asking people to get back to you, it allows them time to decide when they are really ready to engage in discussion.

How to Engage in Conversation with a Stranger

Scenario

Whether it's a fancy Bar Mitzvah dinner, a chic gallery opening, or the barbeque at your neighbor's house, we all find ourselves avoiding the ones we don't know. It's time to change that. Social gatherings can surprise us all, especially if we get out of our comfort zone for a minute or two. If you smile, you're halfway there. Now try these words. You can't go wrong.

Words to Say

"These types of gatherings can be very uncomfortable, so I'm happy to make a new acquaintance. Please tell me a little bit about yourself and what brings you to this party."

Why They Work

By admitting that meeting new people can be uncomfortable for most of us, you immediately increase the comfort level of the stranger. Even the most outgoing and confident person can feel at a loss for words when meeting someone for the first time. By asking that person to tell you a little bit about himself, which people love to do, you have taken the burden of making witty banter off your shoulders. Plus, you'll look like a great conversationalist!

36

How to State a Differing Viewpoint

Scenario

If you really want to be heard, listen first. If you want your viewpoint considered, consider the other person's viewpoint first. If you exhibit listening skills, like not interrupting and reserving judgment, you can ask for the same in return. Whether you're approaching someone with influence in the company or dealing with a more intimate relationship, the need to state a differing viewpoint is something we do all the time. Here are some words to help you get started.

Words to Say

"I hear what you're saying and understand your reasoning and logic, but could I offer a different point of view here to consider?"

Why They Work

When you acknowledge you are listening with a critical ear, and that you understand the other person's perspective, you are in a much better position to ask for the same in return. Stating differing viewpoints requires listening without interruption and then weighing the individual points being made. Ultimately, coming to a satisfactory agreement means everyone gets a little of what they want.

How to Respond to a Disapproving Parent

Scenario

All of us can relate in some way to this scenario. It could be our taste in dating companions, how we're rearing our children, or the jobs we are pursuing. Even the most supportive parents can show their disapproving side at one time or another. Try not to let their words carry too much weight. This response is direct and mature.

Words to Say

"I am not necessarily seeking your approval. I am an adult, and my request is that you trust my ability to make the correct choices for me. I'm the one who has to live with the consequences, and I'm prepared to do that."

Why They Work

Setting these boundaries lets the overbearing parent know that as an adult you are confident and smart about the choices you make. No matter how old we get, many of us deal with a critical or disapproving parent long into our adult years. The parent/child relationship may not have evolved as it should have. Stop your parent short with this no nonsense statement. You can certainly agree to listen to their opinions, but the ultimate decisions are yours.

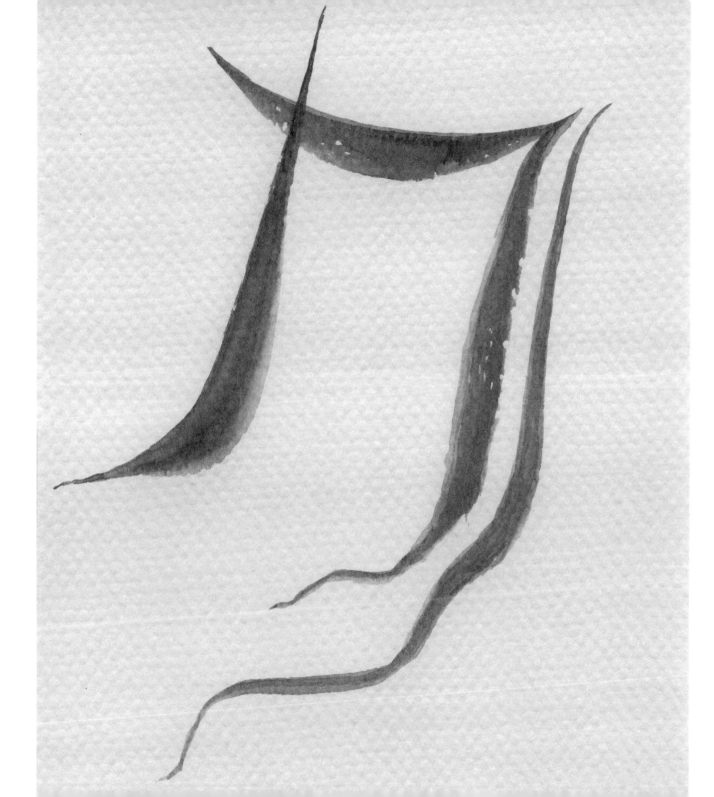

How to Respond to a Friend Who has Experienced a Great Disappointment

Scenario

Your sister calls you crying because she didn't get the job she'd spent three months preparing for, or you find out that your good friend was dumped by a callous lover. What do you do? Disappointment is all around us. How you respond to a friend's disappointment may seem simple, but there are some pitfalls. Avoid the tendency to talk too much about your own similar disappointments. Avoid clichés like, "You'll get over it," or "It just wasn't meant to be." A show of empathetic support is captured in these next words.

Words to Say

"I am so terribly sorry you didn't get the job/your relationship didn't work out like you had hoped. I can see how disappointed you are. If you need to talk, I'm there. If you want to be alone, I'll give you some space. Just tell me how I can help."

Why They Work

Support from friends comes in many forms: listening, comforting, laughing with, acknowledging, affirming, appreciating, admiring. Acknowledging one's feeling of disappointment and showing compassion is a powerful gift. There is no greater sign of friendship.

How to Respond When You Encounter an Ex in Public

Scenario

I imagine there are probably more exes out in the world than current companions, so we're bound to run in to them at some point or other. We often dread the thought of being caught off guard if we happen to see them in public, especially if we've moved on with our life and they seem determined to be quarrelsome. But here are some words to say to that ex without feeling like you have to connect longer than you really want.

Words to Say

"Hi. I had not expected to run in to you, so I'd like to just keep walking and not pretend there's interest in catching up. Best of luck."

Why They Work

These words keep you from having to engage in unwanted conversation or pretense. Your comments aren't unkind, just somewhat curt. Wishing him luck, if you choose to use it, is an appropriate closing because it shows good will, but not too much warmth or emotion.

How to Respond to Receiving Unsatisfactory Service

Scenario

People seem to expect great service all the time. In fact, our standards are getting higher, and our tolerance lower, for the kind of service we expect. As a result, unsatisfactory service is something we all face and have to deal with. We can ignore it and feel like wimps because we did nothing. We can make a scene and see how far that gets us. Or we can use the words here, which can be universally applied to almost any situation.

Words to Say

"I am not at all happy with the service I got today. (List specific complaints: you came late, were unprepared, and you treated me discourteously.) Unless we can come to some agreement on how to correct these problems, I will be asking for a full refund (or I will be speaking to your supervisor)."

Why They Work

The minute you start yelling is the minute people stop accommodating you. Approach unsatisfactory service with an even tone and a prepared list of infractions. By asking how they plan to fix the problem gives them an opportunity to make things right and meet your needs at the same time. Just remember, the uglier you get, the less they want to help you.

III.

EMOTIONALLY INTENSE SITUATIONS

How to Respond to a Verbally Abusive Person

Scenario

Why is it people are so angry these days? It seems like we face angry people everywhere – in our cars, at work, at home, at sporting events, in restaurants. You might be a coach on the Little League team and an angry parent is berating you in front of the crowd. Perhaps a coworker is loudly accusing you of losing a file that you know nothing about, or someone is yelling at you to hurry up in the line at the bank. When we have to interact with these hotheads, it can be the ultimate conversational challenge. The words I am suggesting are particularly useful if you are caught off guard by one of these angry people.

Words to Say

"You must be speaking to me that way because you think you can. Well, you can't, and until you take a kinder tone, this conversation is over!" (Now stop talking or turn and walk away)

46

Why They Work

By asserting yourself, you're letting the angry person know this is going to be a two-way conversation. A bully is taken by surprise with your direct approach and will often back down when he hears your demand. You have also established equal footing with your tone, which allows you the opportunity to guide the conversation in a more constructive direction.

How to Respond When Meeting Your Ex-Spouse to Discuss Visitation or Custody Arrangements

Scenario

The court has ruled. The visitation is in place. It's time to discuss the details. Approach this meeting with maturity, a collaborative spirit, and let the words below get you started on the right foot.

Words to Say

"I really want to try to keep the best interest of the children in mind while we discuss this. If that's okay with you, let's really look at our schedules and see where we might be able to come to some agreement."

or

"If you are willing to compromise a little on the _____, I'd be willing to give in a little on the _____. I know we can come to some agreement that will let us get something we each want."

Why They Work

By showing a willingness to compromise, using a little give and take, you should be able to negotiate some of what you both want. No matter how your marriage ended, a meeting with an ex-spouse can be difficult, particularly when it comes to discussing the children. By really thinking in terms of the "best interest of the children," your ex might be more willing to see you getting away from selfish interests and be more amenable to coordinating time and working together.

How to Ask for a Raise

Scenario

I was on a job for several months and was struggling with how to approach my boss for more money. Grateful to have work, I took the job knowing I was being underpaid. My boss had heard great things about my performance and seen letters by clients and employees singing my praises. I went that extra mile. Now was the time. I decided to get my ducks in a row, determine where I brought value – which we all know is the bottom line – and then with an air of confidence and determination, I used the following words.

Words to Say

"I have brought with me to this meeting a list of the contributions I have made to the company. Besides the obvious ones, such as being on time every day, not being absent, and always agreeing to take on extra work, I have proven over time my value in the following ways: _____, _____, _____, _____, and _____. I'm asking that you acknowledge these contributions with a raise at this time."

Why They Work

Asking for a raise requires diplomacy and conviction. This is a very tricky area. You need to be succinct, yet clear on what you are asking. Enumerate your contributions to the company so your boss sees exactly how valuable you are to the bottom line. By making a request rather than a demand, you leave room for open-minded discussion and more likely an outcome in your favor.

How to Respond When You Do Not Get the Job

Scenario

Finding a job these days is a full-time job. One must be incredibly knowledgeable, persevering, prepared, polished, articulate, and many other things. We follow leads, and then follow some more leads. When we finally get our foot in the door, it can be a very disheartening experience to find out we didn't get the job. Whether you're a jobseeker looking for a different position within your current company or you're seeking external employment, these words can work for each possibility.

Words to Say

"Well, that's disappointing. I had really hoped it would be a good fit. I trust you found someone that will be a real asset to the company. I look forward to meeting him/her."

or

"Well, that's disappointing. I had really hoped it would be a good fit. I trust you found someone that will be a real asset to the company. Could you share with me how I might improve my chances so I can become a more competitive candidate next time?"

Why They Work

Tell them how you feel. It's real. It's truthful. Your graciousness at accepting your fate while wishing the new hire well wins you respect on every level, and asking how you might improve your chances next time shows perseverance and determination.

How to Tell Someone You Do Not Want to Drink Alcohol or Do Drugs

Scenario

We have all found ourselves in this very precarious situation. It may have been in high school or not until college. The pressure to drink alcohol is one of the most dangerous peer pressures we face. No one is immune. In an attempt to get you to drink, you may be ridiculed and made fun of. You may even have your drink spiked. The pressure to drink or do drugs takes many forms. It takes real character and strong principle to stand up to this. Be prepared with these words before you need them.

Words to Say

"Thanks, but I'm not interested. I need to have a clear head right now, and I don't want to risk embarrassing or endangering myself in any way."

Why They Work

If you say it with conviction, you will make it very clear exactly where you stand. This brief statement is useful in many settings. Whether you are at school activities, parties with classmates, or one on one with a persuasive friend, these words leave no room for discussion.

How to Graciously Back Out of a Promise

Scenario

I had a close friend who was going through a horrible divorce and needed to talk. She asked me to join her for a quiet lunch, something we didn't do very often. I promised I'd make time and had every intention of going. As it got closer to the lunch, I realized I would have to cancel due to work commitments. I hated to disappoint my friend, but it just couldn't be helped.

Words to Say

"I want to tell you I made a mistake and overstated what I promised. I'm sorry, but I will have to reschedule the _____. I hope you will understand and let me make it up to you."

Why They Work

By acknowledging and apologizing for failing to keep your promise, you give the one you hurt room to forgive and move on. A promise is a vow, and the recipient of a promise takes it to heart and invests a lot of emotion in your words. I believe you should never make promises lightly. If you break promises often, you're making too many.

How to Respond to a Racial Slur

Scenario

You are sitting in your office when a coworker asks you why they would hire a #$&*%#, or perhaps you are in the company of some crass, bigoted friends who share an off-color remark about a certain race. Either way, you are in a position to respond. You may respond with a nervous laugh or uncomfortable silence, but these are the words that really might stop the comments.

Words to Say

"I know you may think it's okay to say that to me, but I don't. I am uncomfortable hearing such remarks and find them terribly offensive. In the future, I prefer that you don't include me in such conversations."

Why They Work

This statement carries a lot of weight because you are asserting yourself. It takes courage to speak out on this subject. It's easier to let it go. We cringe and say nothing. By saying these words, you are telling the speaker it is crass and inappropriate. You are verbally putting your foot down that you won't tolerate this language anymore.

How to Graciously Refuse a Marriage Proposal

Scenario

You've been going out a while. Things have gotten comfortable and somewhat predictable. There's a connection, but no fireworks. You notice your boyfriend has been fidgety, secretive, nervous—not his typical behavior. You see he's gone to some trouble. The candles are lit. A lobster dinner replaces the usual Ramen noodles. Then all of a sudden he's on bended knee. Yikes! Stop it now before it's too late.

Words to Say

"Wow! I didn't see that coming. If I misled you in any way about where we were headed, I apologize. I never meant to do that. As flattered as I am by your proposal, I'm not ready to make that commitment to you. I'm sorry."

Why They Work

Expressing your surprise diffuses the situation a little. It reinforces your apology by letting the one who proposed know you didn't expect the proposal, nor were you encouraging his offer. Acknowledge that you are flattered, but be unequivocal in letting him know you are not ready for a commitment at this time.

How to Back Out of a Wedding

Scenario

Oooohhh, a wedding! Big sigh.... So many people go through with this life-changing event even when they know in their heart they're not right for each other. They get caught up in family expectations and childhood dreams and often don't look with depth and introspection at the person with whom they're supposed to spend their life. Remember, it's smarter to stop a wedding and suffer the embarrassment and probing questions that will inevitably follow than to endure a bad marriage. Here are some words to help put on the brakes.

Words to Say

"Despite all the planning and preparation thus far, it's important you hear what I am about to say. I am rethinking my commitment to this relationship, and I need to stop the wedding at this time."

Why They Work

By emphasizing how important it is that he listens to what you are about to say, you show the seriousness and immediacy of the situation. There will, no doubt, be ongoing discussion when you say these unexpected words, but these will give you a start on how to take action before the wedding plans become a runaway train.